Easiest Way to Write Your Action Research

Jonny S. Viray, Ed. D.

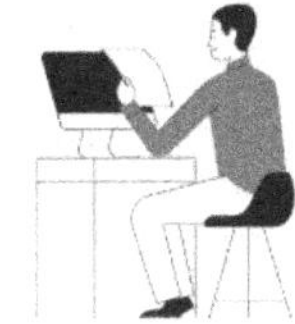

Copyright © 2021 EASIEST WAY TO WRITE YOUR ACTION RESEARCH
by Jonny S. Viray, Ed. D.

All rights reserved. No part of this publication may be reproduced, distributed, or transmitted in any form or any means, including photocopying, recording, or other electronic or mechanical methods without the prior written permission of the publisher and author, excerpt in the case of brief quotations embodied in critical reviews and certain other non-commercial uses permitted by copyright law. For permission requests, write to the publisher at lovelypoetess95@gmail.com.

Published by Poetry Planet Book Publishing House
Arranged by Tess Ritumalta
Edited by Marie Ezekiel
ISBN:
978-621-8261-25-9 – Softbound
978-621-8261-26-6 - Hardbound
978-621-8261-27-3 – Mobile/kindle

FOREWORD

This book is a product of the learnings, experiences and trainings I have related to writing action research proposal.

Despite all the readings and seminars we have, there are times that we are still having hard time to begin writing an action research proposal.

This book provides step-by-step procedures on how to write your action research proposal in easiest way. The goal of the book is not to provide suggestions on how you can transfer your thoughts, learnings and ideas on action research into a manuscript of your own.

The author decided to use simple words to help you complete your action research proposal.

CONTENTS

Research is one of the activities that is said to take much of the time of a person. It is said to be a rigorous work and it is not that easy to convince teachers to write their action research because they already have a lot of work to do that are related to their teaching functions.

Teachers sometimes do not realize that they are already doing action research. They are just not able to put it into writing or have the necessary documentation for it.

When teachers experience problem in their work especially in the classroom, they find ways on how to address them with the best of their knowledge and abilities. Action research tries to provide solution to a certain problem. If teachers are already doing this, the only thing that is needed to be done is to help teachers put everything in paper.

As a solution to the need to capacitate teachers to write their action research, trainings and seminars were given to teachers. Concepts, theories and ideas on what research is all about are cascaded to teachers.

Despite the number of trainings given to them, there are still few teachers who are able to do it. What is missing in some of the trainings is to provide the suggested steps on how the teachers will put everything into writing.

This is main reason for the existence of this book. It will help you write your action research in an easy way by providing the steps needed in every part. The suggested steps may be considered by the teachers as well as the given pattern on how each part may be written.

Parts of an Action Research Proposal

Knowing what are the things that are needed to be accomplished will help a person do the task easier. Having this said, it is very critical to know first the part of an action research proposal.

You may have knowledge about the parts of research based from the trainings that you have attended or the classes in the graduate school. However, there are times that the terms being used in an institution is different from the others. It is their institutional policy. If you are going to check thesis, dissertation or other research, there may terms that are different from the parts of action research.

These are the parts of an action research proposal:

* Title Page

* Table of Contents

* Context and Rationale

* Research Questions

* Hypothesis/Hypotheses

* Significance of the Study

* Type of Research

* Respondents

* Sampling Method

* Proposed Innovation/Intervention/Strategy

* Instrument/s

* Data Collection Procedure

* Ethical Considerations

* Data Analysis

* Work plan

* Cost Estimates

* Plan for Dissemination and Utilization

* References

* Appendices

* A. Instrument/s

* B. Consent and Assent Letters

* C. Declaration of Anti-Plagiarism and Absence of Conflict of Interest

In writing your action research proposal, the text of the manuscript must conform to the following:

Paper Size   :   8.5" x 11"

Font Size   :   12

Font Style   :   Times New Roman

Text Spacing   :   Double Space

Note: You may consider checking the format of your division if there is a boarded to be used.

Chapter I

The Problem and Its Background

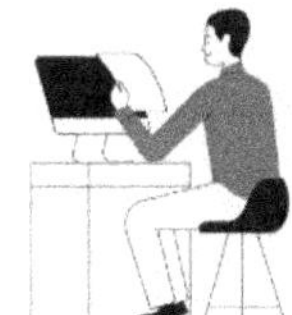

Chapter I or The Problem and Its Background consists of (1) context and rationale, (2) research questions, (3) hypothesis, (4) significance of the study, and (5) scope and limitations.

It tells information primarily about the problem that the researcher intends to solve. Using the five parts, the researcher will provide clear details to the reader about the existence of the problem and how the researcher plans to solve it.

Context and Rationale

The context and rationale plays an important role in writing your action research proposal. This is the part where the researcher presents the situation as well as the problem that the researcher intends to solve.

Furthermore, analysis of the root cause of the problem as well as the proposed solution will be discussed here. Another information that will be seen here is the review of related literature and studies.

To write the context and rationale, the problem to be solved must be identified first using the available data from the school.

Identifying problem may be done through the use of *gap analysis*.

Targets	Actual Data	Gap
MPS English must be 75	MPS in English is 53.25	There is 21.75 gap in MPS in English
Attendance of parents must be 100% duirng general assembly	Attendance of parents is 65.34% during general assembly	34.66% of the parents do not attend on general assembly
100% of the students must be independent readers	78.21% of the students are independent readers	21.79% of the students are not yet independent readers
100% of the learners' materials are given to the students	100% of the learners' materials are not given to the students	100% Grade 8 students do not yet have learners' materials
100% of the students must be numerates	77.33% of the students are numerates	22.67% of the students are not yet numerates

In accomplishing the gap analysis, the researcher needs to check on the documents available in the school like the school improvement plan, report card, accomplishment report and others.

The researcher needs to accomplish the table with *targets and actual data.* Once the information are complete, the researcher just needs to subtract the actual data from the targets to accomplish the *gap.*

You may do your own gap analysis using this template.

Targets	Actual Data	Gap

Note: Get your data from the documents of your school

Once the gaps are identified, the next part is to determine which among the gaps will be prioritized to be solve. Yes, it is beneficial for the school if all of the problems will be given solution. However, since we are starting to learn writing action research proposal, it is suggested to just have one problem to be solved.

To make a decision, which among the problems to be solved, the gap analysis template will help you do it.

The items on the GAP of gap analysis template are needed because these are the pool of problems that we get from the available data.

Decision matrix

Gaps	Doable	Relevat	Urgent	Impact	Total
There is 21.75 gap in MPS in English	5	5	5	5	20
34.66% of the parents do not attend on general assembly	4	4	4	4	16
21.79% of the students are not yet independen t readers	5	4	5	5	19
100% Grade 8 students do not yet have learners' materials	3	4	5	5	17
22.67% of the students	5	5	4	4	18

are not yet numerates					

To do this, you need to copy the gaps from the gap analysis in your decision matrix. You will see on the upper part of the table the doable, urgent, relevant and impact. You may consider these parameters for making decision but you may also have your own parameters. For this activity, we will use doable, urgent, relevant and impact.

From the scale of 1 to 5, provide your score on each gap and parameter. Once it is completed, you may add the scores of each gap for you to determine which is the priority problem to be solved.

In the example, the 21.75 gap in MPS in English is the problem to be solved because it is the

most doable, most urgent, most relevant and will have a huge impact for the school.

You may do your decision matrix using this template.

Gaps	Doa-ble	Rele-vat	Ur-gent	Im-pact	Total

Once you are done with you gap analysis and decision matrix. We will proceed with the root cause analysis for us to find out the main reason for the existence of the problem.

To do it, you will your decision matrix and get the one with the highest because this is the problem that we are going to solve. In the example in this book, "There is 21.75 gap in MPS in English" is the problem that has the highest score and considered as most doable, most urgent, most relevant and will have a huge impact for the school.

We need to begin the root cause analysis with the chosen problem. Doing the root cause analysis, will require you to ask the question "why?"

Root Cause Analysis

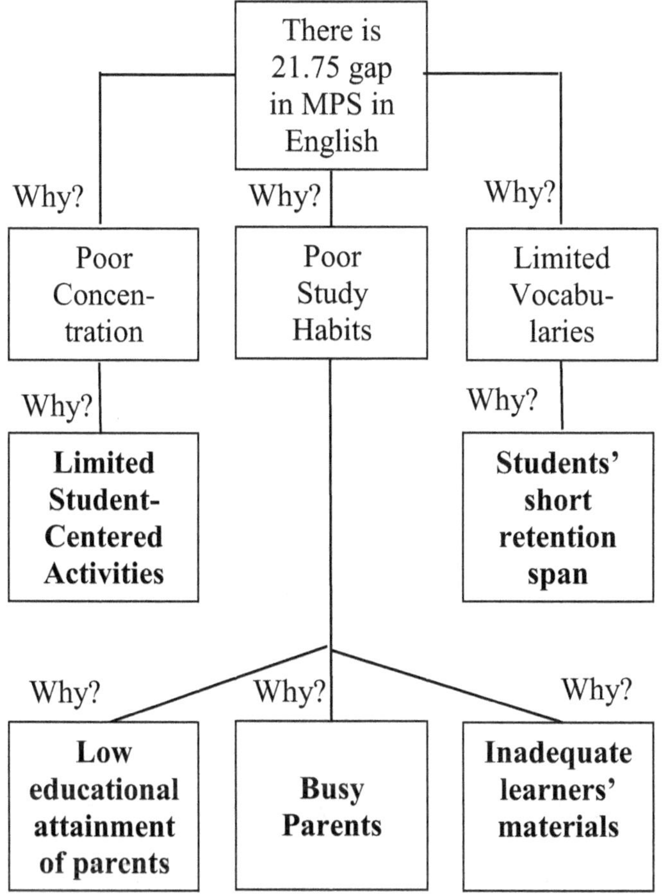

In doing your own root cause analysis, you may or remove boxes depending on what you discover when you answer the question "why?".

The boxes with bold letters are the most important parts of root cause analysis. These are the root causes that is why they are in bold letters for emphasis. From the five boxes, "busy parents" and "low educational attainment of parents" are the root causes that are uncontrollable. This means that teachers do not have control to solve those root causes. This means that we will choose from the remaining three root causes: "limited student-centered activities", "students' short retention span", and "inadequate learners' materials".

From the root causes, you need to analyze which among them is the one that you can solve within your capacity as a teacher or as a researcher.

You may consider using another decision matrix or deeply check on your duties and responsibilities and your capabilities as a teacher.

For this activity, we will choose the "limited student-centered activities" as the root cause that is most feasible to be solved.

You may use this template your doing your root cause analysis.

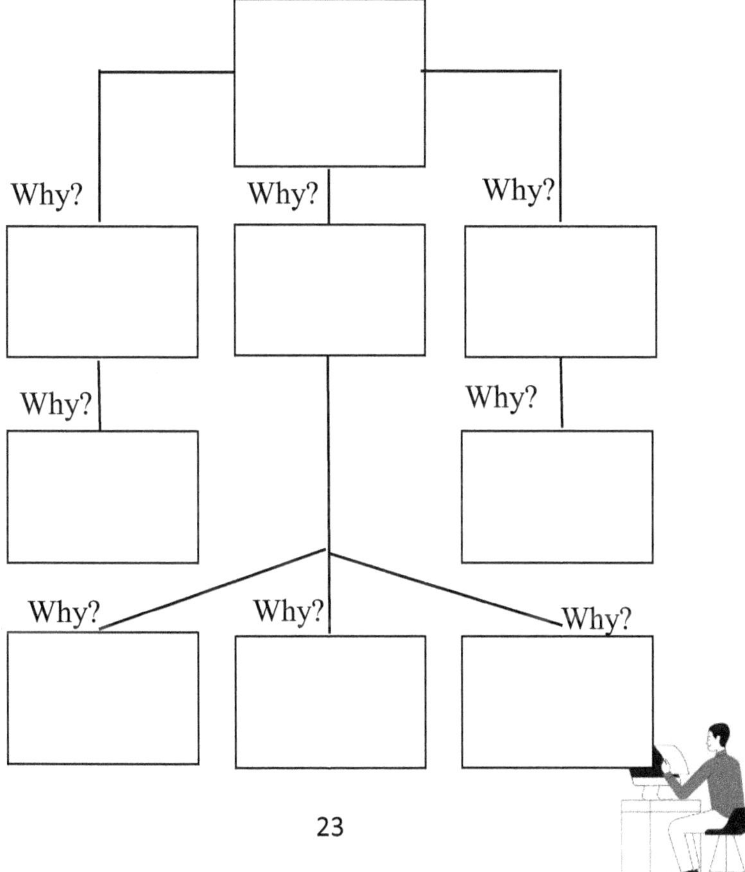

Note: You may add or remove boxes if needed.

Once you are done with identifying the root cause of the problem, we need to provide a solution on the root cause. Going back on the previous activity, we chose "limited student-centered activities" as the one that we will address.

We need to make sure that when we provide solution, we need to match it on the root cause. If the root cause is about instructional material, we will propose instructional material. If the root cause is about motivation, we will propose something related to improving motivation. Since in this study, the root cause is "limited student-centered activities", we will propose a solution that is related to giving student-centered activities.

Once you have already decided that solution that you want to propose to address the problem and its root cause, you must be able to visualize it on your mind on how are you going to use it.

It must be clear for you first what is the solution, what do you need to realize the solution and what are you going to do when you are already using the proposed solution. If these things are vague for you, it is possible that your proposed solution is not feasible.

To address the "limited student-centered activities" in the activity, the researcher will proposed the 4A's method of teaching.

Once we have the problem to be solved, the root cause of the problem and the proposed solution we are now ready to write our context and rationale.

To begin, you need to have the following:

1. decision matrix

2. root cause analysis

3. proposed solution

To accomplish context and rationale, you may use the following steps:

1. List down the problems on decision matrix and grouped the ideas accordingly

2. Use cohesive devices and sources of information to strengthen the claim for the existence the claim for the existence of the problem.

3. Write a statement to show the root cause that you want to solve

4. Present the proposed solution

5. Provide details on what the proposed solution is all about

6. Do a review of related literature and studies and present the gap

Example

1. There is 21.75 gap in MPS in English
2. 34.66% of the parents do not attend on general assembly
3. 21.79% of the students are not yet independent readers
4. 100% Grade 8 students do not yet have learners' materials
5. 22.67% of the students are not yet numerates

We will group them like this:

1. There is 21.75 gap in MPS in English
4. 100% Grade 8 students do not yet have learners' materials
3. 21.79% of the students are not yet independent readers
5. 22.67% of the students are not yet numerates
2. 34.66% of the parents do not attend on general assembly

Problem 1, 3, 5, and 4 are grouped together because these are about students. Problem 2 is separated from them because it is about parents' attendance.

Context and Rationale

27

As one of the complex subjects in the curriculum, teachers are expected to utilize all possible means to make the students master all the necessary competencies, however data of the school magnified that the English Department was not able to attain the target MPS. There is a 21.75 gap between the target and the actual MPS of the learning area. In addition, Grade 8 students do not have learner's materials yet which makes the learning more difficult for them. As known, books are the partners of the teachers and students in their learning journey. What makes it more difficult is that according to diagnostic test, 21.79% of the students are not yet independent readers and 22.67% of the students are not yet numerates.

Learning will be more successful if the parents are always there to support the students.

Unfortunately, 34.66% of the parents do not attend on general assembly.

From the given problems, the "21.75 gap in MPS in English" is the problem that has the highest score and considered as most doable, most urgent, most relevant and will have a huge impact for the school.

As you see from the example, the information from the decision matrix were the ones used in writing context and rationale. The five problems presented were present in writing the context and rationale.

You also noticed other information like "As one of the complex subjects in the curriculum, teachers are expected to utilize all possible means to make the students master all the necessary competencies, however data of the school magnified that the English Department was not able to attain the target MPS." This is additional statement for you to be able to introduce well the problems that you are presenting. You may consider reading other books and research about education for you to have an idea on what you may use to present the problems in your decision matrix.

The last paragraph of the example is also noticeable "From the given problems, the "21.75 gap in MPS in English" is the problem that has the highest score and considered as most <u>doable</u>, most <u>urgent</u>, most <u>relevant</u> and will have a huge <u>impact</u> for the school.". The underlined words here are the parameters we used in the decision matrix to select the problem that we will solve.

Congratulations! You are now ready to begin writing your action research proposal using the guides of this book.

You may begin writing your context and rationale now on your computer or laptop.

Context and Rationale

    Step 1

    Step 2

Context and Rationale does not end with transferring the information from decision matrix to your computer or laptop. To continue writing the it, we will need your "root cause analysis". You just need to present the chosen problem as well as the root causes.

You may consider this pattern:

It was revealed that the "problem" exists because of "root cause that you can solve". As a solution, the researcher will use the proposed solution to improve the "what problem will be improved?".

Example

(3) It was revealed that the gap in the MPS exists because of limited student-centered activities.

(4) As a solution, the researcher will use the 4A's

Activities, Analysis, Application and Assessment to improve the academic performance of Grade 7 students in English.

(5) It is a student-centered teaching strategy that aims to provide an interactive teaching-learning process in the classroom. Teaching-learning process will begin with activities. The activities will be analyzed by the students to discover the knowledge that they need to know. Once they know the lesson already, they will be asked on how they can apply it in real-life setting. Lastly, an assessment will be given at the last part to evaluate the learning of the students.

You may continue writing your context and rationale now on your computer or laptop.

Context and Rationale

    Step 1

    Step 2

    Step 3 and Step 4

    Step 5

Good job!

You are almost done with the context and rationale of your paper. If you use "Times New Roman 12" as your font and "double spacing", you will notice that you are almost at the end of your first page.

It may be hard to write an action research proposal for the past years, but if you have this book, it will guide you to complete your action research proposal.

The next thing to do is to have a comprehensive reading of related literature and studies. There are so many neophyte researchers who are having hard time in doing the review of related literature and studies. One reason is that the variables are not that clear for them.

For a beginner, technical terms of research may hinder your progress in completing of action research proposal. To make it simple, there are two important information that you must always remember when you do your review related literature and studies. In our action research, these are "the problem that you want to solve" and "the proposed solution". These two are your variables. The problem is the dependent variable and the proposed solution is the independent variable. We will focus our review of related literature and studies on these two.

When you search for literature and studies, you may use the internet to have an easy access to the information that you need. You may check google scholar, google, or a reputable website that will provide you access to research, journals and other relevant materials.

However, there are times that limited information are shown by the internet. When you search, you may consider changing some terms when you type in the browser.

You may consider typing these in your browser:

1. research about grades of students

2. research about grades of learners

3. research about academic performance of students

4. research about academic rating of students

5. thesis on grades of students

6. thesis on grades of learners

7. thesis on academic performance of students

8. thesis on academic rating of students

9. academic achievement

10. performance of students

The point is to look for key terms that will help you surface the most relevant literature and studies so you can use them in your action research proposal.

Example

For the past decades, there has been continuous reform in the curriculum and education system of different countries to ensure that they can provide the best education to their learners. According to MolokoMphale and Mhlauli (2014), academic performance of the students is a reflection of the kind of education that is given to them. When students have high academic performance, they are receiving effective delivery of instruction. However, it cannot be discounted that academic performance of the students is affected by numerous factors.

You may continue writing your context and rationale now on your computer or laptop.

Context and Rationale

Step 1

Step 2

Step 3 and Step 4

Step 5

Step 6

Writing your review of related literature and studies is not a one-night work especially if this is your first time doing it. It may require you to read research, thesis or dissertation for you to be able to present well the information that you get from literature and studies.

However, if you are experiencing challenges here, it does not mean that you cannot write your research anymore. You may continue doing the other parts of the research and you may always go back in writing your review of related literature and studies once you are done with the other parts.

The point here is you do first the things that are easier for you to progress in writing your action research proposal. You may also check the attached sample at the last pages of this book for you to have a reference.

Research Questions

This part provides the general statement of the problem and the specific questions of the study. It is also known as "statement of the problem" or "objectives of the study".

Before going on this part, the problem to be solved and the proposed solution must already be clear to the researcher. In addition, the respondents of the study must already be identified.

In writing the research questions, these items are needed:

1. the proposed solution (example: 4A's method)

2. the problem to be solved (example: academic performance)

3. the respondents (example: Grade 7 students)

4. the subject (example: English)

To write the type of research, the following steps may be considered:

1. Provide the needed information on the given pattern for general statement

2. Provide the needed information on the pattern for specific questions

3. Provide your proposed output

Look at this pattern

The main purpose of the study is to determine the effectiveness of ___proposed solution___ on improving the __the problem to be solved__ of _the respondents__ in _the subject_.

Specifically, the study will answer the following questions:

1. How may the __the problem to be solved_ of the control and experimental group be described in their pretest?

2. Is there a significant difference between the __the problem to be solved__ of the control and experimental group in their pretest?

3. How may the __the problem to be solved__ of the control and experimental group be described in their posttest?

4. Is there a significant difference between the __the problem to be solved__ of the control and experimental group in their posttest?

5 What instructional support plan may be proposed based on the findings of the study?

Example

Research Questions

(1) The main purpose of the study is to determine the effectiveness of 4A's method on improving the academic performance of Grade 7 students in English.

(2) Specifically, the study will answer the following questions:

1. How may the academic performance of the control and experimental group be described in their pretest?

2. Is there a significant difference between the academic performance of the control and experimental group in their pretest?

3. How may the academic performance of the control and experimental group be described in their posttest?

4. Is there a significant difference between the academic performance of the control and experimental group in their posttest?

(3) 5 What instructional support plan may be proposed based on the findings of the study?

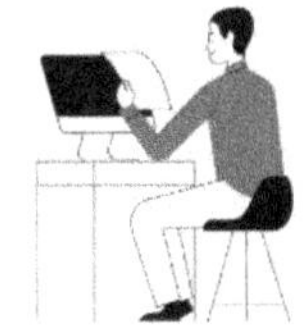

You may write your research questions now on your computer or laptop.

<table>
<tr><td>

Research Questions

</td></tr>
</table>

Hypothesis/Hypotheses

This is the easiest part in the whole research paper. It tells about the proposed assumption of the researcher that is based on the research questions.

To write your hypothesis/hypotheses, you may consider the following steps:

1. Copy the questions on the research questions with the word significant

2. Convert the questions into declarative sentences

3. Convert the positive statements to negative statements

Example

Hypotheses

(1)

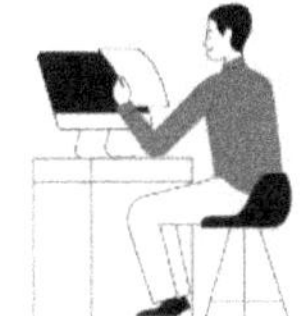

1. Is there a significant difference between the academic performance of the control and experimental group in their pretest?

2. Is there a significant difference between the academic performance of the control and experimental group in their posttest?

(2)

1. There is a significant difference between the academic performance of the control and experimental group in their pretest.

2. There is a significant difference between the academic performance of the control and experimental group in their posttest.

(3)

Hypotheses

1. There is no significant difference between the academic performance of the control and experimental group in their pretest.

2. There is no significant difference between the academic performance of the control and experimental group in their posttest.

You may write your hypothesis/hypotheses now on your computer or laptop.

Hypothesis/Hypotheses

Significance of the Study

This part explains the importance of research or why is it needed to be conducted. It shows who will benefit from the study and how they will benefit from it.

The significance of the study has simple but precise statements when it is presented.

To write the significance of the study, the following steps may be used:

1. Identify who will benefit from the study and arrange them according to hierarchy

2. State the benefit

3. Elaborate its effect to the beneficiaries

Example

Significance of the Study

(1) It is expected that the following will benefit from the study:

School Heads. *(2) The results of the study may help the school heads to attain higher performance indicators for the school through this action research. (3) With this, they will be able to accomplished one of the objectives of their OPCRF to get higher performance rating, which may be used for future career advancement.*

Teachers. *(2) The study may be of great help to teachers to have a teaching strategy that will assist them in their instruction. (3) When teachers adopted the proposed strategy, they may be able to provide better instruction to their students which will be reflected in their classroom observation tool and may further increase their teaching performance.*

Students. *(2) They will benefit the most in this study because of the goal of the research which is to improve their academic performance. (3) Through the 4A's method, they may enjoy more participating in their lessons and may result to better retention of lessons and increase in their scores in different assessment.*

Future Researchers. *(2)The study will be added to the existing body of literature and studies regarding 4A's and academic performance. (3) This may be used by future researchers as reference for future studies. In addition, the recommendation section may also provide the future direction of investigation.*

You may write your significance of the study now on your computer or laptop.

Significance of the Study

Scope and Limitations

The scope and limitations provides information on the place where the researcher will be conducted. It also gives the readers details on the boundaries of the study.

In writing scope and limitations, you may look on the following steps:

1. State where and when the study will be conducted

2. Provide details on the place

3. State the respondents

4. Discuss what will happen to the respondents

5. Delimit the study

Example

Scope and Limitations

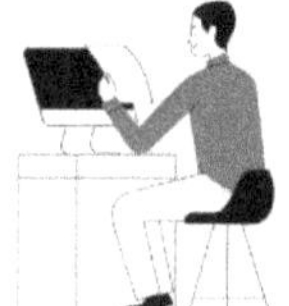

(1) The study will be conducted at AAA High School during the School Year 2019-2020. (2) It is one of the public secondary schools in the Division of XXX where the researcher is currently assigned. (3) Two sections from Grade 7 will be chosen to be the control and experimental group.

(4) The control group will be exposed to conventional way of teaching, while the experimental group will use the 4A's method. (5) The study will be delimited on determine the effectiveness of 4A's method on improving the academic performance of Grade 7 students in English.

You may write your scope and limitations now on your computer or laptop.

Scope and Limitations

Chapter II

Research Method

Chapter II or the Research Methodology includes the (1) type of research, (2) respondents, (3) sampling method, (4) proposed innovation/ /intervention/strategy, (5) instrument, (6) data collection procedure, (7) ethical considerations, and (8) data analysis.

This part deals with how the research will be completed. It provides details on what the researcher will use, apply and do to answer the questions posted in the previous chapter or the research questions. This part must be clearly written to ensure that the readers will have a thorough understanding of the whole process.

Type of Research

The type of research is the first part of the research methodology. It discusses the method that the researcher plans to use. To start writing this part, one must know first the research method to be used.

Since the purpose of this book is to guide you to write an action research, we will use the quasi-experimental design in this activity. Still, it is advisable to study and read other research designs for your own professional development.

To write the type of research, the following steps may be considered:

1. State the research design to be used

2. Define the research design using literature

3. Expound the definition

4. Discuss how it will be used

5. State the reason for choosing the research design

Example

Type of Research

(1) The study will adopt the quasi-experimental design to have a comprehensive presentation of the data to be collected. (2) Thyer (2012) stated that quasi-experimental design involves the manipulation of independent or treatment variable to see its effect on the dependent variable. (3) Through this, the goal of the researcher is to determine the effectiveness of the proposed intervention on the problem being addressed.

(4) The researcher will need to create at least two groups for comparison. One group will be the control group and the other one is the experimental group who will receive the treatment or the experiment. The groups will both be given

assessment before and after the conduct of the experiment to measure if the intervention is effective.

(5) *The rationale for choosing quasi-experimental design is that it suits the purpose of the study, which is to determine the effectiveness of 4A's method on improving the academic performance of Grade 7 students in English.*

You may write your type of research now on your computer or laptop.

Type of Research

Respondents

The second part of research methodology is the respondents. It tells the people that will be involved in the study. Usually, they are the main source of information.

Most of the times, the students or the pupils are the respondents of the study because the main duty of the teachers is to facilitate instruction.

To write this part, you may consider the following steps:

1. State who will be the respondents

2. State the location of the respondents

3. Cite the population

4. State the grouping of students

Example

Respondents

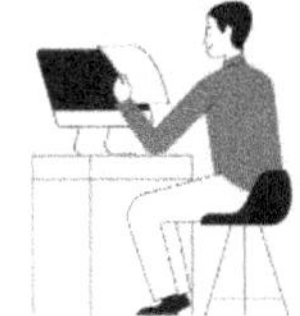

(1) The respondents of the study will be the Grade 7 students of (2) XXX High School during the School Year 2019-2020. (3) Considering the records of the learner information system, there are 437 Grade 7 students who are divided into 16 sections. (4) These students are group heterogeneously to ensure that no section is better than the other.

You may write your respondents now on your computer or laptop.

Respondents

Sampling Method

The third part of research methodology is the sampling method. As the name suggests, it provides information on how the respondents will be selected in a study.

There are different types of sampling technique that a research may use. The major types of sampling are probability and non-probability sampling. Probability sampling is divided into more types as well as the non-probability sampling.

To know these different types, it is suggested to have a reading on these so you may decide on the most suited one for your study.

In writing the sampling method, you may check the following steps:

1. State the sample size

2. State the sampling technique to be used

3. Define the sampling technique based on literature

4. Expound the definition

5. Present a table of respondents

6. Discuss the content of the table

Example

(1) From 17 sections of Grade 7 students, the researcher will consider two groups of students to be the control and experimental group. (2) These two sections will be chosen through cluster sampling. (3) Showkat and Parvin (2013) mentioned that it is a probability sampling technique that gives equal opportunity to everyone in the population to be included in the selection. (4) It is a way that allows the researcher to choose samples from the population based on the theory of probability.

(5) Table 1. Respondents of the study

Table 1 shows the two data about the two groups

Groups	Male	Female	TOTAL
Experimental	17	15	32
Control	18	15	33

(6) It can be seen on Table 1 that experimental group has 17 males and 15 females, while the control group has 18 males and 15 females.

You may write your sampling method now on your computer or laptop.

<table>
<tr><td>

Sampling Method

</td></tr>
</table>

Proposed Innovation/Intervention/Strategy

This part of the research paper focuses on giving details about the proposed solution on the problem that the researcher is trying to solve. It can be an innovation, intervention or strategy depending on the kind of problem that the researcher intends to give solution.

The main goal here is to give readers a clear picture on how the researcher will use the proposed intervention, solution or strategy.

These steps may help you write this part:

1. State the proposed innovation, intervention or strategy to be used

2. Provide details on the proposed innovation, intervention or strategy

3. Discuss how it will be used

Example

Proposed Innovation/Intervention/Strategy

(1) To provide solution on the academic performance of Grade 7 students in English, the researcher intends to use 4A's method. (2) It includes Activities, Analysis, Application and Assessment. It is a student-centered teaching strategy that aims to provide an interactive teaching-learning process in the classroom.

(3) As the name suggests, the presentation of the lesson will begin with activities rather than the usual discussion of the lesson. The activities to be given in class will be used as spring board for the analysis stage. When these students do the analysis, they are trying to discover the lessons on their own with the guidance of the teacher. Once the content of the lesson is already clear to the students, they

will be asked to provide situation on how they can apply these learnings in real-life situation. Lastly, an assessment will be given at the last part to evaluate the learning of the students. This teaching approach will be used in experimental group for one grading period.

You may write your proposed innovation/intervention/strategy now on laptop.

Proposed Innovation/Intervention/Strategy

Instrument

It refers to the tool that the researcher will use to gather pertinent information that will answer the research questions or the statement of the problem.

It is critical for the researcher to determine the most appropriate instrument to be used in the study. The researcher needs to base the decision on the problem that he intends to solve.

If the problem is on poor attendance, the instrument to be used is the tool for checking of attendance.

Since in this study, the we are trying to solve the problem on academic performance, a test or examination may be given to the students to measure their academic performance on a specific subject.

Once you have decided on the instrument to be used, you may also consider these two things:

1. You may adopt a standardized or pre-validated instrument that is suited on your study

2. You may also have a researcher-made instrument, but it will be subjected to validity or reliability check

Either of the two will do. You just need to make sure that the instrument is suited on what it intends to measure.

The following steps may be considered to help you write this part of research methodology:

1. State if you will use researcher-made or adopted instrument

2. Describe the instrument

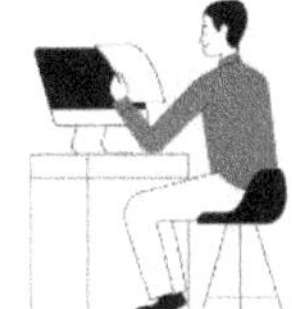

3. Provide details on the validity/reliability of the instrument

Example

Instrument

(1) The researcher will adopt the standardized test in Grade 7 English of the Division of XXX to measure the academic performance of the students. (2) The instrument is a pen and paper test, which is crafted based on the competencies prescribed in the curriculum guide. It has 50 questions that can be answered through multiple choice.

(3) It is crafted by the expert in the division and it underwent series of revisions and validation. Since it is validated, it can already be used by the researcher.

You may write your instrument now on your computer or laptop.

<table>
<tr><td>

Instrument

</td></tr>
</table>

Data Collection Procedure

The data collection procedure tells how the researcher will gather the necessary information for the study.

To put it simply, it tells the story on how the researcher plans to start and end the study. As much as possible, the researcher will help the reader to visualize the scenario by giving complete details on data collection.

However, the data collection procedure depends on the research design or type of research used in the study.

In this action research, the following steps may be adopted to write the data collection procedure:

1. State the time frame

2. State what will happen with the two groups

3. State the date of pretest

4. State how long is the exposure

5. State the date of posttest

Example

Data Collection Procedure

(1) The researcher will check the DepEd Calendar for the School Year 2019-2020 to plan the data collection. (2) Within this time frame, the experimental group will be exposed to 4A's, while the control group will be exposed to conventional way of teaching.

(3) On the first day of third grading period, the two groups will be given a pretest. This is needed to measure their baseline characteristics before the actual conduct of the experiment. The scores on the pretest will be subjected to statistical

treatment to determine the comparability of the two groups.

(4) From this point, the whole grading period will be used to expose the control group on conventional way of teaching and the experimental group to 4A's.

(5) On the last day of the grading period, the posttest will be given to measure the academic performance of the two groups.

You may write your data collection procedure now on your computer or laptop.

Data Collection Procedure

Ethical Considerations

This part shows that the researchers will abide to the laws and adhere to requirements of conducting a study.

It also shows that the researcher does not intend to bring harm to anyone before, during and after the investigation is completed.

You may check on these steps in writing your ethical considerations:

1. Ask the permission of the school head

2. State that it will be forwarded to Division Office

3. Inform the district research coordinator

4. State students that will not be informed

5. State that data will be treated confidentially

Example

Ethical Considerations

(1) Before the full implementation of this study, the researcher will seek the approval of the school head. (2) Once this is secured, it will be forwarded to the Senior Education Program Specialist in charge of Planning and Research in the Division of XXX. (3) After getting permit from the Division Office, the district research coordinator will be informed about the intent of the teacher to conduct a research. (Step 3)

(4) Students in the control and experimental group will not be informed about the research to avoid Placebo, John Henry and Hawthorne effect. Still, consent of the parents to allow their children to be part of the study will also be secured. (5) Lastly, all the data collected and identity of the respondents will be treated with utmost confidentiality and secrecy.

You may write your ethical considerations now on your computer or laptop.

Ethical Considerations

Data Analysis

This is the last part of the research methodology that gives the reader the information on how the data will be treated. For an action research, it usually tells the statistical treatment of data.

Majority of the researchers now are using software for statistical treatment. Still, it is advisable to consult someone who is knowledgeable on this part for you to determine the most appropriate statistical treatment to be used.

The questions to be answered and the data to be collected may help to determine the statistical treatment suited for your study.

You may check on these steps in writing your ethical considerations:

1. State if you will use a software or assistance of licensed statistician

2. Provide details on the statistical treatment to be used

Example

Data Analysis

(1) Descriptive statistics, statistical analysis and SPSS (Statistical Package for Social Science) computer program will be used to analyze the data in order to ensure valid and reliable interpretation of results.

The following statistical treatment will be used in this study:

1.   Mean will be used to measure the academic performance of the control and experimental group.

Mean Range	Description
41-50	*Outstanding*
31-40	*Very Satisfactory*
21-30	*Satisfactory*
11-20	*Needs Improvement*
0-10	*Poor*

2. T test will be used to measure the significant difference between academic performance of the two groups.

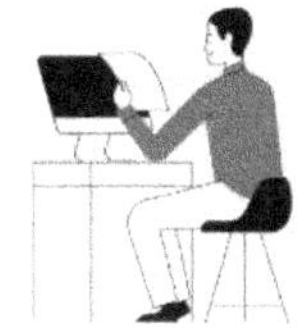

You may write your data analysis now on your computer or laptop.

<table>
<tr><td>Data Analysis

</td></tr>
</table>

ABOUT THE AUTHOR

Sir Jonny S. Viray is a public school teacher at Masantol High School, Masantol, Pampanga since 2013. As a public school teacher, he gives importance on providing his students enjoyable learning experiences inside and outside the classroom.

His father is a pedicab driver and worker in fish port, while his mother is a plain housewife. Growing from a poor family, he wants to serve as an inspiration to his students and other children. He believes that a person can always change his life for the better.

REFERENCES:

MolokoMphale, L. and Mhlauli, M. (2014). An Investigation on Students Academic Performance for Junior Secondary Schools in Botswana. *European Journal of Educational Research*, 3(3)

Showkat, N. & Parvin, H. (2013). *Non-Probability and Probability Sampling*. Researchgate.

Thyer, B. (2012). Quasi-Experimental Research Designs. Oxford University Press.

MolokoMphale, L. and Mhlauli, M. (2014). An Investigation on Students Academic Performance for Junior Secondary Schools in Botswana. European Journal of Educational Research, 3(3)

Regional Memorandum, 57 s., 2018. Reformulated Regional Research Agenda Version 2 and Call for Research Proposals

Showkat, N. & Parvin, H. (2013). Non-Probability and Probability Sampling. Researchgate.

Thyer, B. (2012). Quasi-Experimental Research Designs. Oxford University Press.

Sample Action Research

Scan the QR Code

or go to this link:

bit.ly/samplear1and2

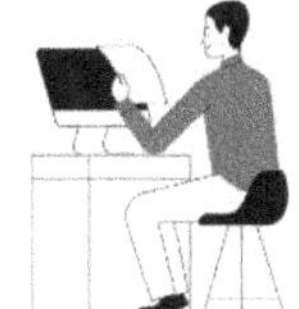

www.ingramcontent.com/pod-product-compliance
Lightning Source LLC
LaVergne TN
LVHW020925200726
843506LV00011B/1815